How To Be a GIRL!

How To Be a GIRL!

(An A to Z Guide for Tweens!)

Julie A. Martin & Kiki Fluhr

Rocket & Just LLC

First edition published in 2018.
Printed in the United States of America.
ISBN: 978-0-692-15861-6
Library of Congress Control Number: 2018958278

Book design by Julie A. Martin
Photographs © Julie A. Martin
Research and text by Kiki Fluhr
Editing by Julie C. Stephenson
Sponsored by James Donnelly

For information, ordering and permissions, address:

How To Be a GIRL!
Rocket & Just, LLC
howtobeagirlbook@gmail.com

www.howtobeagirlbook.com

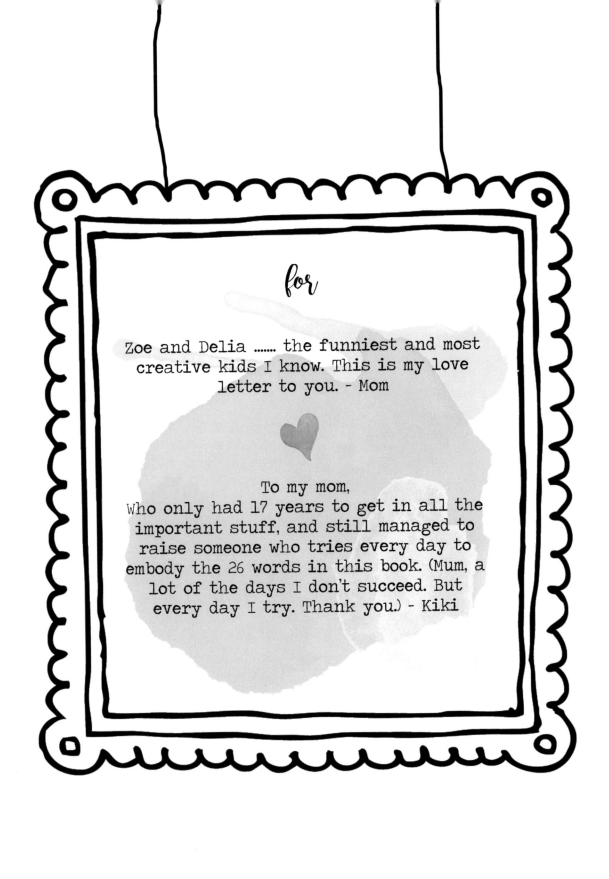

for

Zoe and Delia ……. the funniest and most creative kids I know. This is my love letter to you. - Mom

To my mom,
Who only had 17 years to get in all the important stuff, and still managed to raise someone who tries every day to embody the 26 words in this book. (Mum, a lot of the days I don't succeed. But every day I try. Thank you.) - Kiki

This book belongs to:

_____

"You are more powerful than you know; you are beautiful just as you are." - Melissa Etheridge

A

Adventurous

willing to take risks or to try out new methods, ideas, or experiences; bold, daring, dauntless

Mae Jemison
(1956-present)

Have you ever wondered how you become an astronaut? Mae Jemison was the first African American woman to travel in space, and this was her fearless approach to getting there:

She loved science and asked questions about everything, turning her daily life into a chance to make discoveries. (When a splinter got infected, she did an experiment to find out about pus! Ew, but also kind of awesome, right?)

She refused to get discouraged when people told her she couldn't do something. In her engineering classes in college, she was not taken seriously and was often ignored, both because she was a woman and because of the color of her skin. Instead of giving up, she was unshrinking in her work to prove them wrong.

She dedicated herself to her studies, became a doctor, and served in the Peace Corps.

Most importantly, Mae never doubted for an instant that she would get to travel to space.

NOW Challenge

Write about one exciting thing you would like to do one day. Imagine yourself doing it, and describe how it makes you feel.

Little Musings

If you could go anywhere you haven't been before, where would you go?

b

Brave

showing courage

Malala Yousafzai
(1997 -present)

When Malala was growing up in Pakistan, it was illegal for girls to go to school. Although she knew it was dangerous to speak out against the ruling party, Malala voiced her opinions. At the age of 11, she was blogging for the BBC about life under the control of the Taliban. While shooting a documentary for the New York Times in 2012, she was shot three times and almost killed. Even after almost dying for speaking up, she was intrepid in her fight for girls' education worldwide. At the age of 17, Malala went on to become the youngest recipient of the Nobel Peace Prize ever!

"I don't want to be remembered as the girl who was shot. I want to be remembered as the girl who stood up."

NOW Challenge

Is there something you would like to try, but are scared? What about it scares you? What would make you feel confident to try? Define your fear.

Little Musings

What qualities do you have that make you brave? Who is the most courageous person you know or have read about?

C

Confident

sure of oneself; having self-assurance about one's own abilities or qualities

Corey Maison

(2001-present)

Corey Maison spent the first 11 years of her life "sad and angry all the time," until she figured out what was wrong. She had been born with a male body, but she knew that she was a female. Corey found the fortitude to make the transition from male to female, knowing it would be a really tough road. She knew she would face bullies of all ages telling her she shouldn't be allowed to be her true self.

But she did it anyway, helping people to understand that gender does not define a person and that judging others is really uncool.

"I used to hide behind a fake smile, but now all my smiles are genuine. It feels so good to be MYSELF, and it feels even better to love myself!"

Little Musings

What is it in life that makes you feel really successful and good about yourself? How did you gain that confidence?

NOW Challenge

Build someone up today!
Give out 5 random compliments.

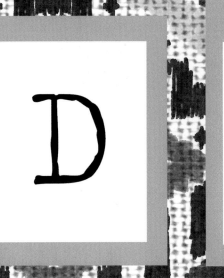

D

Dependable

trustworthy
and
reliable

Susan La Flesche Picotte
(1865-1915)

Susan La Flesche Picotte was a Native American born on the Omaha Reservation in Nebraska. When she was young, she saw a white doctor refuse to treat a Native patient, because the patient wasn't white. This became the turning point in her life - she was the first Native American to become a doctor. She not only treated patients in her village, she was the sole physician on the entire Omaha Reservation - over 450 miles! She saw over 1300 patients, often traveling by horseback in freezing weather over the harsh terrain.

With the help of donations, she opened her own hospital on the reservation. She also went to Washington D.C. to fight for better healthcare for Native Americans, and spent much of her time teaching her people how to stay healthy.

NOW Challenge

Offer to help someone who needs it. Do the dishes without being asked or babysit a sibling to give a parent a nap!

Little Musings

Do you know someone who is always true to their word, that you can always count on? Are you that reliable person for someone else?

E

Empowered

To make (someone) stronger and more confident, especially in controlling their life and claiming their rights.

Chimamanda Ngozi Adichie
(1977 - present)

Chimamanda Adichie is an author from Nigeria, who has put into simple language why every person should be a feminist (someone who believes men and women are equal. Seems like everyone should be one, right?!)

In 2017 she wrote a short book called Dear Ijeawele, or a Feminist Manifesto in Fifteen Suggestions. It began as a letter to a friend who had asked how to raise her daughter to be a feminist, to truly believe she is equal. Chimamanda had some ideas we can all use. Play with trucks as well as dolls. Read a lot, about all different things. Know that difference is totally normal - not everyone is the same. Don't mold yourself to fit anyone's expectations. Being liked by others isn't important. The important thing is to like YOURSELF.

(Side note: Please read this book. It is simple and wise, and a blueprint for how to be a kick-ass woman!)

NOW Challenge

Girl Power! Help someone learn one of your special skills, tutor a child in a subject you excel at, or let your unique personality shine by being a mentor to someone else!

Little Musings

Do you feel empowered as a young woman to reach your goals in life? How can you empower someone else?

f

Focused

directing a great deal
of attention, interest,
or activity towards
a particular aim

Simone Biles

(1997-present)

You might remember
Simone Biles as the
all-around Gold medalist for
gymnastics at the Rio Olympics in
2016. But did you know she holds 19
medals, 14 of which are Gold, for International competitions? That's the most gold
medals for any gymnast, ever! Did you know
she was adopted? Or that she has ADHD (Attention Deficit Hyperactivity Disorder, a
brain difference that can make it a lot
harder to stick with a task)? She didn't
let any of that get in the way of her
goals.

She loved gymnastics so much that
she focused all her attention on
working towards being the best
that she could be. She trains at
least 32 hours a week!

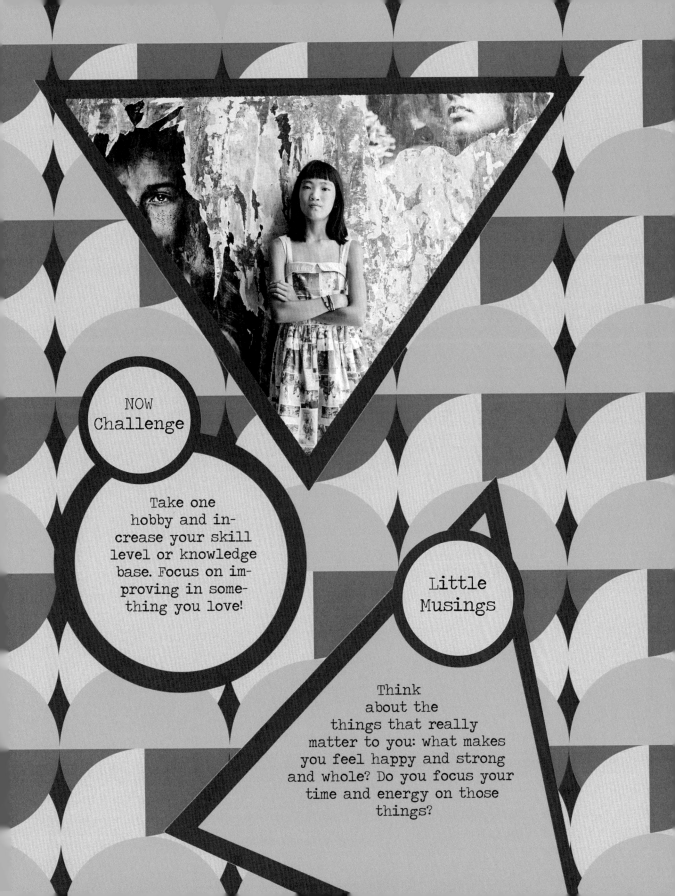

NOW
Challenge

Take one
hobby and in-
crease your skill
level or knowledge
base. Focus on im-
proving in some-
thing you love!

Little
Musings

Think
about the
things that really
matter to you: what makes
you feel happy and strong
and whole? Do you focus your
time and energy on those
things?

g

Generous

showing a readiness to give more of something than is necessary or expected

Oprah Winfrey
(1954-present)

Today, Oprah is a billionaire, the owner of an entire media empire, and one of the most influential women in the world. But she grew up very poor, sometimes with no running water or electricity. She also suffered from regular abuse from the ages of 9-14, but that didn't stop her. Her journey from really difficult beginnings to world-changer was built on little more than willpower, charisma, perseverance, and confidence.

Oprah has been more than generous in sharing her financial success. She has given over $400 million to charities, including those she founded herself. She started a Leadership Academy for Girls in South Africa - a boarding school for girls that often come from extreme poverty, growing up in thatched huts, with no schools or opportunities nearby. After 10 years, some of the school's graduates have become doctors, lawyers, and scientists! She has changed the course of thousands of girls' lives. Her generosity will continue after she dies. Her will leaves $1billion to various causes.

NOW Challenge

Have some money in your piggy bank? Try buying a meal for a homeless person or giving some to a charity!

Little Musings

Name 3 ways you can be generous that don't require having or spending money.

H

Honest

free of deceit; truthful
and sincere

Ava DuVernay
(1972-present)

Only 4% of the directors of the top money-making
films from 2007-2017 were women. Isn't that ridicu-
lous? To make it as a woman director you have to
be 10 times as amazing and 10 times as fierce as
any man. Girls, meet Ava DuVernay.

In her documentary 13th, she is a modern day
truth-teller, trying to get to the heart of what it
means to be Black in America. She explores what
words like "person" and "freedom" really mean.

For work on her film, Selma, Ava DuVernay was the
first Black woman whose film was nominated for
an Academy Award for Best Picture.

And maybe you've seen the movie, A Wrinkle in
Time? We have Ava DuVernay to thank for that one,
too!

NOW Challenge

Tell someone you admire how much you look up to them and why.

Little Musings

Do you find honesty hard sometimes? How do you feel when people are honest with you?

i

Innovative

introducing new ideas; original and creative in thinking

Sangeeta Bhatia
(1968-present)

Are you sitting down? You might want to sit down. This bioengineer has invented a robot that is 1000 times smaller than the width of a human hair, that can circulate inside a human body, and detect cancer. It can detect cancer up to a decade before it would be large enough to cause symptoms, and this early detection could potentially save millions of lives.

Oh, and she's also working on growing miniature livers in her lab, that could be used by people that needed liver transplants!

Dr. Bhatia holds several patents, has co-authored a textbook, and won numerous awards and honors for her work.

NOW Challenge

Think of a problem you want to solve in your own life. How might you solve it? Draw a diagram or picture to illustrate how your idea may work.

Little Musings

Do you think seeing everyday things in new ways can encourage new ideas?
(Stand on your head!)

J

Just

based on or behaving according to what is morally right and fair

Ida B. Wells
(1862-1931)

Seventy years before Rosa Parks made history, Ida B. Wells refused to give up her seat on a "whites only" train car. She was 21, and it took 3 men to carry her off.

She also ran a newspaper, founded the NAACP, and was a leader in the suffragette movement, working to get all women the right to vote!

She was the leading force in ending the practice of lynching: killing someone publicly, without a trial, for crimes or slights that were unproven. She is considered the mother of the civil rights movement, as well as the mother of 6 humans. She was amazing! Go read more about her!

NOW Challenge

Is there a child at school that gets bullied?
Sit with them at lunch, and strike up a
conversation!

Little Musings

What are some injustices
that you see in the world?

k

Kind

having or showing a friendly, generous, and considerate nature

Ellen DeGeneres
(1958-present)

Ellen is one of the most charismatic, joyful, and just plain NICE celebrities there is. She's had a daily television talk show for 14 years, where she's made her case to millions of viewers to really just try to love everyone. She teaches her viewers to be kind to everyone and to not judge anyone based on who they love, or the color of their skin, or how much money they have.

When Ellen told the world she was gay, it opened the door for many others to also be publicly true to themselves. She has given away $21.6 million to charity, and $35 million to viewers of her show. How's that for kind?

".... I want to be an example that you can be funny and be kind, and make people laugh without hurting somebody else's feelings."

NOW Challenge

Make someone's day today! Leave a happy note in a friend's locker. Bake cookies for the mail carrier. Tell your teachers how much you appreciate them!

Little Musings

Has someone shown you a great kindness? How did it make you feel? How can you be kind to others?

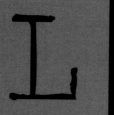

Luminous

glowing; full of light; bright; enlightened; clear

Anne Frank
(1929-1945)

IMAGINE. You are 13 years old. You are hiding quietly in an attic with your family. You are hiding because your own government doesn't think you belong in your country. And all just because you are Jewish.

Now imagine for TWO years, you can't go outside. You can't feel the sun on your skin.

This was life for Anne Frank. She used her journal as an escape from daily life, writing and rewriting about her thoughts, her everyday activities, and the events happening outside in the world that were keeping her hidden inside. When you read it, you can feel the light shining out from her, despite her circumstances.

Eventually her family was discovered and taken to a work camp, where she later died, like millions of other Jews during that period in history. Her father was the only survivor of their family. When he discovered her diary after the war was over, he had it published, so her luminous spirit could live on.

NOW Challenge

Write down 5 positive things in your life right now. Remember those when you are having a hard day.

Little Musings

Do you sometimes find it difficult to see the good, when everything seems to be going wrong?

m

mindful
conscious or aware of something

Amandla Stenberg
(1998-present)

You might recognize her as Rue from The Hunger Games. But she will be legendary because of her voice and her words. Even though she is still a teenager, she has become an international symbol of all a young person can do. She uses her public presence to remind people about things that really need to change.

She used a school project to make a video - "A Crash Discourse on Black Culture" - about what's wrong with cultural appropriation, and it's been viewed 2.3 million times. That's potentially 2.3 millions minds shifted!

"What would America be like if we loved Black people as much as love Black culture?"

NOW Challenge

For one week be extra aware of everything around you, everywhere you go. Do you see anything that you feel should be changed?

Little Musings

Is there something happening in the world that just seems wrong to you? How can you be a positive voice for change?

N

Nurturing

help or encourage the development of someone or something

Maria Montessori
(1870-1952)

Are you a fan of sitting still and listening? Or repeating the same type of math problem over and over? Most kids aren't!

Maria Montessori was a teacher who totally invigorated the educational system, by demonstrating that children learn best by figuring things out for themselves. She had the idea to create a school environment that allowed children to follow an open-ended path and focus on what THEY were interested in, at their own pace, without direct interference from adults.
Kids of all ages are in the same classroom and there are no "grades" in Montessori schools! Maria Montessori wanted kids to LOVE learning and feel good about discovering their own answers.

NOW Challenge

Nurture your environment today! Plant seeds in paper cups and transfer them to an outdoor garden during the Spring.

Little Musings

What helps you feel nurtured and supported? What can you do to nurture yourself?

Patsy Takemoto Mink
(1927-2002)

Today we know that girls can do anything boys can do, right? That wasn't always what people believed.

Some colleges didn't accept girls. Some textbooks only showed men being in charge and making decisions.

And some schools didn't have any opportunities for girls to play sports. (Can you imagine?!) This changed with the passage of a law called Title IX (read, Title 9). It was written by the first woman of color elected to Congress - Patsy Takemoto Mink.

She was Japanese-American, from Hawaii, and she was voted into office for 12 terms! She also worked tirelessly for equal rights and economic justice. But her success in helping to achieve gender equity is what makes her a political superhero!

Little Musings

Do you have a friend or parent that loves something you don't understand? Ask them about it!

NOW Challenge

Read a book about a culture or religion you know nothing about. Seek to understand another's point of view that differs from your own. You don't have to agree with another person's belief to try and understand it!

P

Passionate

having, showing, or caused by strong feelings or beliefs

J. K. Rowling

(1965-present)

Of course you know she wrote the Harry Potter books. But, did you know that while she was writing them, her mom had recently died, she was unemployed, extremely poor, suffering from depression, and raising a baby girl all by herself? All true.

She didn't allow her circumstances to affect her enthusiasm for writing an amazing adventure story. She channeled her difficulties into her book - you can see her sorrow over losing her mom in Harry's own despair, and the dementors were based on her feelings of depression.

J. K. Rowling used to be a billionaire because of Harry Potter. Want to know why she isn't a billionaire anymore? She gave away SO much money to charity!

Because SHE used to be poor, she now has her own charity to help poor families with only one parent. How awesome is that? It's always wonderful to use the memory of your own hard times to encourage you to help other people in the same situation.

Is there a cause or project you feel passionate about?
See if you can get others excited about it too!

Little
Musings

What do you feel excited about that you want to do
all the time?

Harriet Tubman
(1822-1913)

Harriet Tubman was a silent superhero, a spy for the Union Army, a rescuer who saved dozens of people from slavery, a fearless secret agent that snuck hundreds of miles through enemy territory leading others to freedom - not once, but 19 times!

One of the main conductors on the Underground Railroad, she escaped slavery herself in 1849, but was not satisfied. She kept returning to the South to lead more slaves to freedom. They traveled a path through a series of hideouts and safe houses called the Underground Railroad, constantly evading mobs that wanted to kill them, dogs that were trained to sniff them out, and people that would have happily turned them in. She used stealth, smarts, secrets, and disguises to help over 200 people escape, and she was never caught!

NOW Challenge

Learn to say "hello" and "thank you" in a different language. Play a memory game to train your brain to remember things quickly.

Little Musings

Do you solve problems in life quickly and with confidence, or do you prefer to thoughtfully take your time to feel good about decisions?

Respectful

feeling or showing deference and respect

Dorothea Dix
(1802-1887)

Do you know anyone who has a brain that works differently? Perhaps they have autism, or depression, or Down Syndrome. Today, we know this doesn't mean these people are less valuable or important. It only means they are different, and different can often be really great! But in the past, people didn't understand that the way we do now. People with mental illness or with learning differences weren't well understood, and they were imprisoned under horrible conditions. Like in JAIL. Only, they hadn't done anything wrong.

Dorothea Dix lived during that time period. After working in some of these institutions and seeing that the "patients" were often treated much worse than criminals, she helped create the first mental institutions in the U.S., fighting for respectful treatment for those she served.

We are still fighting to de-stigmatize differences today, but she was the first person to make it her concern. She fought for those that could not fight for themselves.

NOW Challenge

Have a conversation with a parent or guardian about what respect means. Does your parent feel like you respect him/her? Does he/she respect YOU?

Little Musings

Is it possible to disagree with someone and still respect their beliefs and decisions?

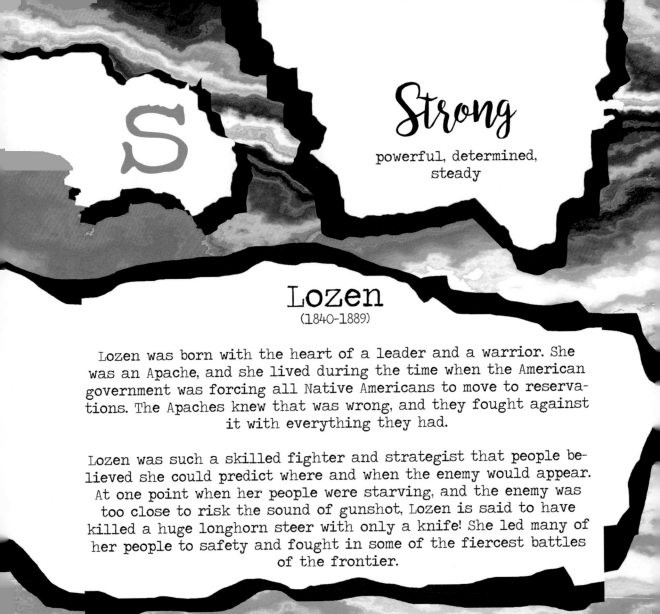

S

Strong

powerful, determined, steady

Lozen
(1840-1889)

Lozen was born with the heart of a leader and a warrior. She was an Apache, and she lived during the time when the American government was forcing all Native Americans to move to reservations. The Apaches knew that was wrong, and they fought against it with everything they had.

Lozen was such a skilled fighter and strategist that people believed she could predict where and when the enemy would appear. At one point when her people were starving, and the enemy was too close to risk the sound of gunshot, Lozen is said to have killed a huge longhorn steer with only a knife! She led many of her people to safety and fought in some of the fiercest battles of the frontier.

Do you think it takes a strong person to admit when they've made a mistake?

Little Musings

Is there an area in your life where you tend to back down? Make a plan for how you can hold your ground next time that happens. Write it down, so you can remember your goal.

NOW Challenge

Tenacious

not readily relinquishing a position, principle or course of action; determined

Dolores Huerta
(1930-present)

Dolores Huerta was a legendary activist for the poor, concentrating specifically on farm workers in the American southwest. She led Labor strikes and helped negotiate better working and living conditions for some of America's poorest workers. In 1972, she created the phrase, "Sí se puede" which means "Yes, it can be done!" It is a slogan used to inspire continued protest even when the odds seem hopeless. Teacher, labor leader, founder of the United Farm Workers Union, and mother of 11 children, her life embodies that slogan, for she has never given up.

"I couldn't tolerate seeing kids come to class hungry and needing shoes. I thought I could do more by organizing farm workers than by trying to teach their hungry children."

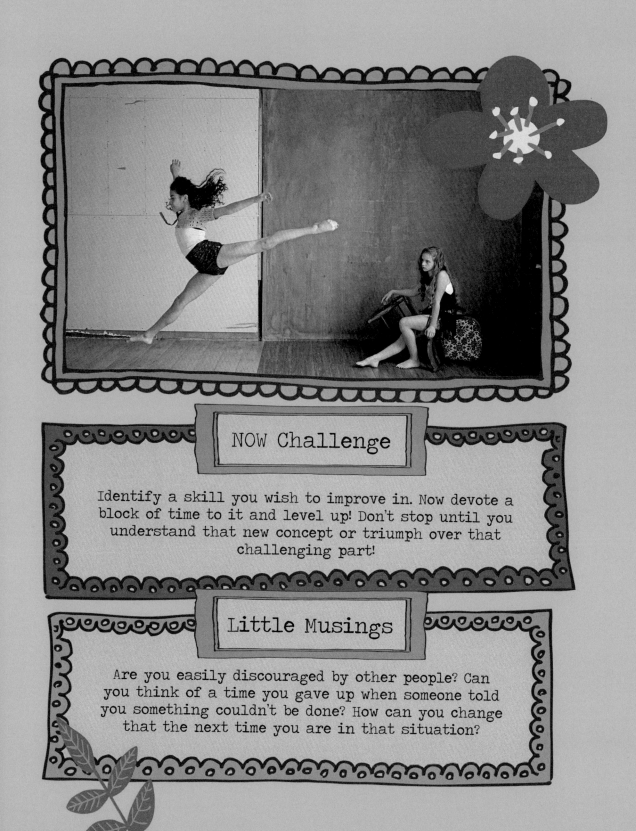

NOW Challenge

Identify a skill you wish to improve in. Now devote a block of time to it and level up! Don't stop until you understand that new concept or triumph over that challenging part!

Little Musings

Are you easily discouraged by other people? Can you think of a time you gave up when someone told you something couldn't be done? How can you change that the next time you are in that situation?

u

Unconventional

not based on or conforming to what is generally done or believed

Coco Chanel
(1883-1971)

Chanel turned the fashion world on its head by saying "nope" to the era's traditional corsets and ultra-constrictive dress. Imagine clothes that were designed to tighten and compress your waist to make it as small as possible, making it difficult to do anything active, or even take a deep breath. Yeah, no thanks.

Things men got to wear - pants (amazing, right?!), flat shoes (hallelujah!), suits, crewneck sweaters - she re-branded them all for women. In the process, she changed people's ideas about what it meant to dress like a woman. Think about that - she altered the world's perception of femininity.

"The most courageous act is still to think for yourself. Aloud."

Do something today that YOU want to do, regardless of what others think is cool.

Little
Musings

Is there something you are interested in that may seem strange to your friends and family?

Victorious

having achieved a victory;
triumphant

Aimee Mullins

(1975-present)

Aimee Mullins was born without shin bones and had her lower legs amputated when she was only a year old. Rough start, right? No big deal. She used that misfortune to turn herself into a kind of superhero! She has accomplished some amazing things in her life, like working as an intelligence analyst for the Pentagon when she was only 17. She won a full academic scholarship to Georgetown University, and was the first double amputee to compete in NCAA track and field. She has set world records in the 100m, the 200m, and the long jump. Aimee has worked as a fashion model and has acted in several movies. And she is an amazing speaker who talks about body image, women and sports, and how adversity can be a great teacher.

And guess what? Her prosthetic legs are modeled after a cheetah, (for real, a cheetah!!), and she can change her height between 5'8" and 6'1" depending on what prosthetics she wears. How cool is that??

NOW Challenge

Write down one goal and tape it above your bed, so you can see it every night before you go to sleep and every morning when you wake up!

Little Musings

What do you think it is that helps people to overcome problems and challenges?

W

Wise

having or showing experience, knowledge, and good judgement

Ruth Bader Ginsburg
(1933-present)

Ruth Bader Ginsburg was wise enough to know that women were just as smart, tough, and capable as men, long before this was common thinking. As a lawyer, a judge, and finally a Supreme Court Justice, she fought and argued hard for gender equality - for women and men to have the same rights and opportunities, and for their wants and needs to be equally valued. She wrote such a wise, convincing argument for women earning equal pay as men, that the President and the Congress changed the law. She literally changed the world with a well-worded argument!

Little Musings

What is one piece of advice that you would give to adults? Do you think adults forget what it's like being young?

NOW Challenge

Have a chat with an elderly family member or friend. What wisdom have they gained in their life that they can pass on to you? What is one thing they wish they had known or understood in their youth?

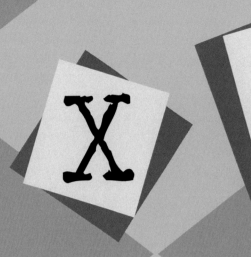

X

eXtraordinary

very unusual or remarkable

Beyoncé

(1981-present)

We all know Beyoncé is extraordinary, but it's the way she wields her fame that is helping to change the world!

After Hurricane Katrina hit New Orleans, Beyoncé started the Survivor Foundation to help people who had lost their homes. She and her mom started a center in New York where people can learn new job skills, to help them have a better life. She also contributed to a project called "Chime for Change", which works to fund education programs for women and girls.

She uses her song lyrics and videos to tell the stories of strong, independent Black women, pushing back against centuries of stereotypes. She is helping pave an easier path for those coming after her, and helping to define a more truthful story we can tell ourselves about race and equality and the awesomeness you can achieve when you simply refuse to fail.

NOW Challenge

Research someone you think is extraordinary. How did he/she become so amazing?

Little Musings

If the story of your life became a movie, what would be the most exciting part? How would it end?

Youthful

young or seeming young

Marley Dias

(2005-present)

When Marley Dias was 11, she was really annoyed with the books she was reading in school. As an African-American girl, she was frustrated that the books "...were all about white boys and their dogs." So she decided to do something about it. Think about that! She was complaining to her mom, and her mom said, "So what are you gonna do about it?" Can we all just take a pause to think about how awesome life would be, if we each did this every time we wanted to complain about something??

Marley created #1000BlackGirlBooks - a campaign that encouraged people to send her books starring black heroines, which she planned to donate. Not only did she reach her goal, she got thousands of people talking about the issue of diversity in literature. Don't we all want to read a story about someone we can relate to? And she's already written her own book: Marley Dias Gets It Done: And So Can You!

Do you think kids can change the world just as much as adults?

Write down 3 of the coolest things about being a kid. Now find a small container and make a time capsule! Open it in 20 years!

Z

Zealous

great energy or enthusiasm in pursuit of a cause or objective

Nellie Bly
(1864-1922)

Nellie Bly loved finding out the real truth, and would stop at nothing to figure it out. She was an investigative journalist, famous for working undercover to get her story. She was convinced that mental health patients were not being treated well, and she was absolutely right! In order to get the full scoop, she had herself committed to a mental institution to write about conditions there.

For another story, she was investigating political corruption in the Mexican government. She found out about so much corruption that she received death threats and was chased out of the country!

As if all that wasn't enough, she held patents for two inventions, and she set a world record when she traveled around the world in 72 days!

NOW Challenge

Share your passions with others today. Invite someone to learn about something you love. Painting? Music? Sports? Video games?

Little Musings

Is there an activity or subject that excites you? Can you see yourself doing that for many years? Write down ways you could make a career out of it!

Made in the USA
Columbia, SC
29 November 2018